A SHORT TREATISE
ON MORTALITY

A Short Treatise on Mortality

NEW POEMS

DOUGLAS REID SKINNER

UHLANGA

2022

First published in Durban, South Africa by uHlanga in 2022
UHLANGAPRESS.CO.ZA

Distributed outside southern Africa by the African Books Collective
AFRICANBOOKSCOLLECTIVE.COM

ISBN: 978-0-620-98689-2
Editing, cover design and typesetting by Nick Mulgrew
Proofread by Karina Szczurek

Cover image © revel j fox, 2021

The body text of this book is set in Garamond Premier Pro 11PT on 15PT

ACKNOWLEDGEMENTS

There are, in the work of any writer, the shadows of many other figures, both personally known and known through their works, alive and dead. I am indebted to them all and grateful for the various kinds of contribution they have made to this book. Without the bricks and mortar of their influences and contributions, this house could not have been built. In particular, I am grateful to Nick Mulgrew for his insightful editorial prompting.

Thanks are due to *Carapace*, *New Contrast*, *Il Tolomeo*, the *...Africa!* anthologies, *Stanzas*, *The McGregor Poetry Festival* anthologies, and any other journal or anthology unnamed through oversight or forgetting, for the first publication of versions of some of the poems included.

– D.R.S.

CONTENTS

Rungs

Over time you grow
from simple body into mind,
losing rungs on the ladder
step after step you've climbed.

I

POETRY

A Short Treatise on Mortality

for Robert Morgan

One of Brodsky's favourite notions was
that a poet's real biography was his poetry.
SOLOMON VOLKOV

Why wake up if you can't light up? asked Brodsky.
Indeed. Death is a downside, one might argue,
to which he'd reply, *A mere inconvenience,*
the dice rolled, non importante, *to be ignored*

when unruly words are there to be wrangled
and there are puzzles that are yet to be solved,
when cups of coffee are waiting in line to be gulped
and poems need scribbling on envelopes and slips;

when a holy smoke lit before venturing forth
raises a cloud above the mind to establish
a proper perspective (well, for him, in his way),
and if less time alive is the price that is asked

by the ever-so-fickle, sweet goddess of song,
why, he'd reach for his wallet and pay without
a moment's hesitation or smidgen of doubt –
not for him, insurance and annual check-ups

as prayers to the deity of our future days,
the modern equivalents of solemn invocations
clung to for keeping the brute Time at bay,
ever skulking in shadows and sharpening its blade.

Why wake up if you can't light up? asked Brodsky,
yet the animal on its treadmill rises regardless,
sniffs out its toast and redolent cup of coffee
before dying without warning in the middle of a thought,

or while gazing from a window across the East River,
or while sitting alone and at odds with the world,
surrounded by smoke and slashing at ghosts,
while assaulting all dicta and counterfeit gods.

.

In the Labyrinth

Diagnosis brought to mind a missed thread, a minotaur
and an ageless story, thought's twists and turns, the floor
threatening to rise up in rebellion against the law

of unassuming trust in the stable nature of things.
The world seemed awry, a host of whirling wings –
no infarction or stroke, but a wholesale loss of bearings.

The doc at the Daedalus Clinic simply did not know
what to suggest, leaving me baffled by the slideshow
the walls had become. *What to do? Where then to go?*

Downtown A&E was the only option. How strange
to drive when all the streets are trying hard to rearrange
themselves in odd ways. After a quick exchange

with the nurse, a portly consultant at the head of a knot
of medical juniors loudly exclaimed, "What you've got,
old son, is a mythical story. Nurse, give him a shot

in his behind. That ought to steady things again."
Jab done, I was parked on the side for two hours of Zen.
Who invented such discomfort, counting sheep to ten

and ten again without sleep? And who on earth
imagined that humans could recover in such a dearth
of peace? But the drugs kicked in and a nurse with mirth

relented and proffered a pen. "Where do I sign?"
Time was blurred and I'd lost my grip on rhyme.
Heading for the exit with my head mostly back in line,

fragments of a word kept echoing... *labyrin... labyrinthine...*

Diagnosis

I keep wondering, 'What's the point?'
CJ DRIVER

A pheasant came into the garden.
It seemed lost, uncertain what to do
about the dog behind the glass
insisting it was worth a bark,
wanting at it, wishing to dishevel
its gaudy, Beau Brummel look,
to deconstruct the meat of it.

It took nothing more than a handle
rattled twice for the bird to get
the message and swiftly scarper,
smacking the air as hard as it could
to gain enough lift over the hedge
to the safety of next door's lawn –
a friendlier place, perhaps.

Thwarted, the dog wandered slowly
towards its bowl, glancing back
as if to say, *Enough with all
the dry stuff, I need choice cuts* –
doing what dogs and children do
in their most appealing moments
with wide and guilt-inducing eyes.

How strange is our predicament,
being ill at ease without a cure
in sight. You walk into the sea
or jump from a height, but what cares?
The loops just keep on running.
We think that thought's the *sine qua non*
and far too easily do we forget

unthinking existence is the main theme.

Two Minutes

We tend to think about things
on the limited scale of our lives,
which are not much more than hamlets
in the wide and dark landscapes of time.

Because each of us in our bounded brains
is tethered to a horse and crocodile
that happily go about their business,
not giving a fig for the Johnny-come-lately

frontal lobes of which we are so proud –
the mountaineer standing beside a flag
on the windy summit for a couple of minutes
(just time enough for the photo op)

before carefully heading back down again
to twinkling lights and soup and bread
and the ever-finer gradations of argument
our croc-horse-human species cannot

avoid engaging in day and night.
And even as she heads back down
towards the air that brims with oxygen,
she knows that there's no certainty

the atmosphere won't turn on her,
won't pause and pivot, won't go all rogue,
that cold and snow and harrowing wind
won't close all routes she has for home.

We tend to think about things
on the limited scale of our lives,
which are not much more than hamlets
in the wide and dark landscapes of time.

Bricolages

to make some one thing
that will not, one knows,
in time, remain.
CHRISTIAN WIMAN

You'd need many hands on which to count
those who through the years have taught
me how to lay these bricks and build
the rooms in which I now must live.

I've talked and watched, watched and talked,
with them and then with many others,
working with patience through the years,
laying brick after brick in practice runs,

learning you cannot practise too much
and that you cannot practise too often,
that it takes those years to figure it out,
to discover what to keep and what discard,

work out how to get the overlaps right,
put in ties, do the corners and bonds,
tap and adjust, tap and adjust, then point
and brush for the final, finished look.

Now, as I walk along strange streets,
I sometimes stop and look at the walls,
going back in mind to work out how
the brickie managed to get it just so,

what mix of sand and cement was used,
what thought and care was paid to it.
You learn your craft from many views
and come to know that precious little

lasts longer than our own short lives.
In the end, the past gives way so that
the new can climb up into air and light –
all the walls I'll not be there to view.

Traces

I was seventeen when I began to learn
how to hold a plough steady and straight
while guiding the horse with whistles and clicks
to keep the share cutting steadily through
the layered soil while aiming for a spot
on a fence or a tree, on a distant hill.

That was almost fifty years ago.
No matter how often you go to plough,
getting the lines right as seasoned men
would want them has always been a struggle:
neat as a choirboy's fresh-combed hair,
great flocks of birds working the soil.

I never meant to spend my days that way.
I had dreamt of travelling everywhere.
Instead, I've studied earth and air,
each change of tension in the ground,
the furrows left when ploughing's done,
the dust that's settled on hedgerows,

the steps from one side to the other,
the hidden creatures living below.
I've stood on corners, haloed by light,
counting the open, breathing lines,
the furrows waiting to be unreeled,
absorbing knowledge from the fields.

Whatever I know I've learned by years
of walking alone in the company of horses,
in mists at night or under the sun,
teeth gritted tight or humming a song,
figuring what's needed for every line.
Who'll look to them when I am gone?

Who'll walk the day and hum in tune
with hoof and share? The traces are
all I've known, their leathers have left
slantwise grooves on back and shoulder.
Even in dreams, they never let go.
In sleep I hear the sibilants calling,

calling for lines to be cut in a field.

In Two Minds

for Lynthia

What you see is a hand with a pencil moving,
and below it a page laid on a table,
lit by a pool of light from a lamp.

The hand is making marks on the page,
going back and forth, line after line,
and leaving behind it as it goes

a scene with a house and hills and sky –
not a drawing, but lines of words in rows
that are the keys to imagining

the scene of a house and hills and sky,
the story that she's conjuring in
your mind as you follow along behind,

word after word as you wander along
and follow behind in her conjured time
the marks she's set on the page in lines,

dark marks in rows inside your eyes,
dark marks aligned within your mind,
dark marks that go on happening in time

in the pool of light lying on the page,
on the page that's looking at your mind,
your mind and hers combined in signs,

marks made for you to find in lines,
marks made to become the keys to conjure
a house and trees and hills and sky,

a scene that's held in mind and time
as you follow a pencil, trailing behind,
as you watch her make the marks in lines

that conjure hills, a house and sky,
and know while watching from on high
that page and marks set out in lines

are in your eyes and in your mind,
your mind and hers now wholly aligned,
going on, going on, a song in time.

Out of the Blue

So many years had to disappear
before you found the book once more
that kept you glued one night for hours
to where you'd found the poem you felt
that you would always rue

because it seemed so perfect then
and seemed to frame near everything
that the author had wanted to say.
If only it was me, you'd mused,
if only I could write that way.

And then one day while searching through
bookshelves for something to distract
you come across that book again
and feel your way right to the page
where still it's there to taunt and flay

because you've yet to find a way
to sit and wait, to wait and pray
as she once did throughout the day,
to try and tame a tangled mind
that would not stay, stay in place

until, at last, one thing that's true
would unexpectedly arrive
and coalesce straight out of the blue –
although (you know) she knew that it
would always take much more than that

and many further bartered days,
would cost much more for her to tame,
until it had become the poem
you read back then, now see again:
with not one word that you would change.

An Epistle to T Voss in Sydney

I bought *The Puncher & Wattmann Anthology
of Australian Poetry* last week, edited by
John Leonard (rev. 2020). You see,

I never kept up after Les Murray's radical
Oxford book in '86 that shocked a few,
so I've opened up space in my chock-full

days to have a read of who is doing what
Down Under. Or, perhaps, who is and was
doing what. Or, at the very least, the part

of the tapestry Leonard thought was worth
showing strangers of who is and was doing what.
Over four hundred pages arrived. Such girth

is daunting, like a great big, busy beehive.
You know there's sure to be sweetness inside,
but it's crowded, and you wonder before you dive

which of them will help you get your fill.
You just have to take the whole buzzing lot on,
hoping your cover of feigned expertise

gets you past the words, each ready to sting
whoever is trying to get at the honey,
each ready to die for the language queen.

Step aside, you argue, *I have business here.*
You hope to get stung, only not too much.
Everything smells of eucalypt and acacia.
The thrum of wings sounds like a burgeoning wind.

Words

Bored witless with overuse
and so many anonymous mouths,
they're inclined to tee off and start
beating up on you just for the fun.

So, you shout, *Do you mind?*
I'm trying to get through the day unscathed
and I don't need all your crap.
Piss off and leave me alone.

Not a bit of it, though, and instead
they crowd in a bunch and start kicking
so hard the dust flies in a cloud
thick enough to choke a poor camel.

You don't know if it's best to yell out
or to roll yourself into a ball.
You cannot ignore what they're doing,
pretend that nothing is happening –

that's when they really apply themselves,
try to pound you into a pulp.
Sod this for a game of soldiers, you say,
and run flat out for the corner...

around which you encounter a gang
of arguments and swaggering contradictions
trip-wired and loaded for trouble,
for the fun of back-alley fisticuffs.

So you freeze – *Jeez Louise, I give up!* –
and that's when the oddest thing happens.
Just at the point when you simply let go
all of your knotted mental muscles,

your assailants take to paring their nails
or sighing and drifting away,
leaving you breathless and shaken,
sweat cooling and night coming on.

You're miles from where you were headed,
you're late to where you were going;
the air's getting cold and you're feeling old,
and there's still a long way to go.

Uninvited

She just walked in through the door one day.
I'd never seen her before and didn't have a clue
where she was from, though she seemed
vaguely familiar and resembled others

I'd known in earlier years – that shade of hair
when caught by sunlight in just such a way,
how she'd pause and slowly purse her lips,
or raise an eyebrow and look right through you.

Not sure what to say, I mumbled a question,
asking whether or not she'd be staying over.
She answered without answering and left me
to figure out what might lie in the future,

to prepare for years of ongoing uncertainty.
Every time a question has come to mind,
her response has left three more in its train.
Some appear to have no answer at all

and I can't stop looking at her and wondering
what might be next, or might change on any day,
if the one who strolled nonchalantly indoors
would later still be there in front of my eyes,

or if she would be someone so different
it would leave me utterly puzzled (or elated).
She's still here, now, before me, dressed
in layer after layer of meaning, always skirting

my continuing questions, evading all probing
for a simple answer, for a clue to her origins,
never fully revealing what it is she has come for,
why in this strange universe she keeps appearing,

always smiling, enigmatic, and inviting.

Poetry

I've seen you loitering on the corner again.
You ditch me for months – *years* – then reappear,
expecting me to swan around with you, that I can
just be picked up where you left off and went silent,
stopped scratching in the half-light with a rusty nib.

You can't. By now you know it's all or nothing with me,
not just when it suits you to put on your dancing shoes.
This is a lifelong adventure, buddy boy, nothing less,
and it costs everything you have to give, and then some.
That's the deal. You know it's so. Don't feign it.

There are no rewards except my embrace, my curves,
the shape of me when you run your hands up and down
in search of a formula, again and again, only to discover
there isn't one. There never has been. Everything is new.
Learning to let go is the trick. I'll do the lifting for you

as long as I have your undying allegiance, your love.
With that in hand, I'll let you loiter all day long.

The Placeholder

Each day becomes its own placeholder –
there you were, or someone much like you
(but not a simulacrum),
in the now that you were in,
someone who seems quite familiar
(but not an exact copy).

Each evening, you faithfully put
a marker between two leaves,
showing exactly where the day ended
(and you with it),
knowing precisely where the next day's circus
will begin (and you with it).

Each morning, you carefully take it out
from between the sheets
(where it slept for hours),
where it dutifully kept your place
and kept your time
(while another self was dreamed).

Each day becomes its own placeholder,
a dance of light and shadow
in which looking back you might hope to find
a familiar you, but not a copy,
not a simulacrum –
a marker between two dreams.

Tightrope

If I did not believe that somehow or other
this would reach you, that it would
arrive intact, in one piece, as expected,
that it would find its way to where you sit,
arrive where you sit and wait,
where you have always been
sitting and waiting for it to arrive,
waiting for what's never been before,
for what you've never seen before,
for what you've always been
waiting for all this time,
for all these years, on your own;

if I did not know you would be there,
would be waiting there for it to arrive,
how could I continue,
how could I keep on going,
how could I go on doing this,
go on believing and making
– *poised tiptoe on Time's tightrope* –
how could I keep you in the mind's eye,
how could I possibly hold you there,
keep you poised and waiting right there,
waiting with open hands and eyes,
sitting alone and watching,
waiting for a knock or a ring,
waiting to rise and walk across the floor,
waiting for footsteps to arrive at the door?

If I did not see, could not see,
were I unable to see that somehow or other
this would reach you where you are,
that it would arrive there, in one piece,
would reach your waiting hands and eyes,
would reach you exactly as expected,
how could I sit here, poised all day
on a tightrope, waiting,
for what I've never seen before,
for what I've never known before,
for what I've never been before?
How could I keep on watching and waiting,
looking through windows,
looking at the sky, poised and alone,
waiting alone for the shimmering moon
to come searing up and flood the room?

It Became a Song

When eventually, after all the plodding years,
he looked up from the page, night had fallen,
lights had come on up and down the street,
and he understood that there it was, at last,
hewn from the very wood he had been stuck in.

Wandering around perplexed, asking directions
of those passing, or standing still, closing his eyes –
he'd tried it all – even lying down on the lawn
with arms spread; growing a beard; not washing
or repairing where the thread had unravelled.

Violence and words solve nothing, he thought.
The tutelary axe he'd carried for all the years
had become too much to bear. It was wanted
by no one, or no one would take it off him.
And he couldn't just leave it lying around.

The first blow had sent a shock through his arms
as he'd not known how to hold it correctly –
letting your shoulders relax, allowing the weight
to make its own pendulum, gently swinging
back and forth until the time is right.

It became a song: the swing, the swing... and bite.
The swing, the swing... and bite. His body changed.
New muscles appeared and his mind sharpened.
Each morning he abandoned sleep with alacrity,
measured the space around him with fresh eyes,
picked up a pencil, and walked back into the wood.

A Bedtime Story

*Perhaps literature is always repeating
the same things in a slightly different tone.*
JL BORGES

He tried for all he was worth –
gritted his teeth, furrowed his brow –
in a furious effort to grasp
just why it should all boil down
to an open and utterly empty field
followed by carnage and poems,
the mournful cries of far-off curlews,
landscapes revealed by the light of stars,
lightning dancing out of the clouds,
and all of it right in front of his eyes,
inevitably to be followed by
another field, one devoid of flowers.

He stuck at it for the longest time.
Ribbons and keys kept wearing out,
but nothing else seemed worth a sou
for the difficulties of getting down
faint semaphores from an only ever
imagined future, one never known.
What a pickle. To be bookended by
the inscrutable and the inscrutable.
And squawk all you like in the night –
the sooner you get used to it, *amigo*,
the sooner you get used to it.

Misdirection

Such dreams can nag at you something rotten
throughout the morning – the way
they rearrange the normal order of things
called by light and shadow to be the world
we imagine each day into being.

Puzzled, he wondered how it was possible,
when heading alone in a car for the coast,
that the sign should have an arrow pointing
straight ahead for the town of Stellenbosch,
with Elgin to the right, below it on the post.

He eased the wheel over to take the corner,
sensing that it might just be the way to go...
but over a rise he found the car heading
down a steep hill, with a village on the slope,
each red-roofed house neatly in its row.

How did they get here? he asked himself,
slowing to a crawl. *And why is no one about?*
He knew there ought to be rutted dirt roads
through fruit trees as far as the eye could see,
so he pulled to the side, set the brake and got out...

Which is when the familiar world returned,
the bedding all lying in a heap on the floor
and early light painting patterns on the walls.
I never seem able to get where I'm going,
no matter where it is that I'm aiming for.
Invariably, I end up here, instead.

The Cost of Poetry

It seems as if each poem completed
(wrapped in brown paper and tied with string)
replaces some piece of one's anatomy –
a patch of skin for a line, a vein for a lyric,
part of an organ, perhaps, for the book
that purely by accident happens to get
a restless audience up onto their feet.

Long hours of reading once bolstered the form,
while transfusion and transplant kept a supply
of words flowing deep and into the suburbs.
But now they must go, they've served their time,
like the stitched-on extra ear for hearing
each snap of dry twig in the understory
signalling that something's about to happen.

The body limps on, here half an inch gone,
there, a slight failure of function the cost.
All weight once gained could perhaps be bartered,
or a kidney might prove enough for a trade.
The dark liver, it's said, regenerates itself
if you drop the muse and consoling booze –
though what does that leave one to live for?

At supper one night in the town of Padua,
the poet Zanzotto read poems for an hour
to an audience who'd come from far and wide.
At seventy-five, he seemed quite fragile,
as if running out of substance to sacrifice.
Even so, his old eyes told of deep resolve
to go on doing what would cost his life.

The Book That's Now Being Read

According to my Auntie Meg –
not an actual aunt, but my mother's best friend
from when they studied nursing back then –

the day before my parents were to wed
my mother called in a state to say
she just wasn't able to go through with it.

She'd woken that morning and realised
they wanted different things from life.
Distraught and crying, she was, she said,

convinced that she had to call it all off.
It took a half-hour to calm her down
and see the trouble she was likely to cause.

They were married just as it had been planned.
An old photograph shows them arm-in-arm
outside the church in Port Elizabeth.

My father's standing in his dress uniform,
my mother has pearls around her neck,
holds a tussie-mussie in her hand.

My sister wondered aloud one morning,
"But what if she hadn't telephoned Meg,
or Meg hadn't managed to convince her

that they really had to go ahead with it?
Or she'd caught a train to the Cape instead
and had only phoned the following day?"

"Then you and I would never have been,
would never have been alive or dead,
and I most certainly wouldn't have written

the book that's now being read."

2

AFTER

A Riposte

to CJ Driver's 'Manifesto', in which he embraces iambics

Si os dan papel pautado,
escribid por el otro lado
JUAN RAMÓN JIMINEZ

Well, there is cause indeed for us to spend
an afternoon, at least, with lots of wine
 – it must be red, you will agree – and just
a little cheese put on a dry *biscuit*
to keep one's *estomac* at ease while talk
and thought go circling round and round what's lost
or gained by sticking to iambic feet, iambic feet...

I cannot say if it is fair to use
a bit of French to keep the metronome
en pointe. I have no doubt you'll have your say.
I know, the boy employed to drum and keep
the band of many marching feet in time
cannot afford to trip or skip a beat
and yet... We humans, variable as the weather,

need *une goutte* more leeway wherein
to range without too much impediment –
not quite *vers libre* (an oxymoron fashioned
by the ill-advised who couldn't have known
the future would cast it as a grand excuse),
but that which can accommodate the spread
of natural ups and downs – more how we speak.

And so, I'm for the occasional change of beat,
slight shifts of gear, here or there, with room for
dactyls, weighted pauses and amphibrachs, or
occasional spondees chucked in for fun,
to string things out before the end must come –
that symbolic terminus of lines and self
as, like a book, you're shut and returned to the shelf.

Old School

from and for Johann

Those hands that linger in your lap
while eyes take in the distant hills
remember when they once belonged
to a younger man who had woken one day

to find himself returned to where
it all began, the *Cabo da Boa Esperança* –
though perhaps it was the sailor, Diaz,
who named it best when calling it

the *Cabo das Tormentas*, the place
where almost every word dements
and thoughts can test you to despair,
writing out what years are left,

enclosed in language, never sure
just what of us can possibly endure –
unable to redeem your fears despite
fame's blandishments and grand awards,

a deepening shelf of fragments shored.

Out of Breath

after Elizabeth Bishop and for Tony Voss

The loss of your art grows faster and faster
the older you get, and the waning of intent
leads to a point where it seems like disaster.

You try for new lines, keep trying to master
the silence, the echoes and all the years spent,
yet the loss of your art grows faster and faster.

You practise each day and keep going after
pure lines that beguile on love and Tashkent,
but it always ends in what seems like disaster.

After only ten lines you're doubled in laughter,
the oxygen of hope hissing out of the tent
as the loss of your art grows faster and faster.

You breathe ever louder, petition the hereafter,
but the lines have dried up, you're utterly spent
and the half-empty page seems just like disaster.

With hope's oxygen hissing straight from the tent
you crumple the page, wonder where it all went...
as the loss of your art grows faster and faster,
and leads to a point where it seems like disaster.

The Deep You

Miraculously returned to speech,
if not to life, the great Alan Turing
in the form of a voice coming from a machine

opines to the poet who keeps sweating away
on night after night and page after page
of figures, symbols, lines and verses,

that the day would soon be upon her
when there'd be no way at all of saying
whether or not a poem she had written

had in fact been written by him
in his current flickering incarnation,
for by then he would know off by heart

every poem that had ever been published –
how it works and to what it's related,
and how one might write so many more

in just such a mode, or style, or voice,
in any of the possible futures to come.
He would be, he said, wholly in tune

with Dante, John Milton, TS Eliot,
William Yeats, Rimbaud and Auden.
By comparison, your senescence, he suggested,

will be marked by a growing awareness
of the darkness that looms for each one of you.
So, don't bother, he gently encourages,

let me take on the lifting and I'll carry the load.
I'll hum and I'll blink, and no one will know
it was me and my 'fingers' tapping the keys

while you smile and relax, there just for the show.

Written

after Eugenio Montale

I

Some details we know, retained from the flux:
that he'd wait on his own in the cold and the fog,
strolling back and forth to keep himself warm;
that now and then he would cough to clear his throat.
We know he'd buy newspapers and hardly read them,
describing them as not being worthy of the name.
That he smoked Giuba cigarettes, later banned,
as he walked up and down. That he was never sure
if she'd arrive, or if the train had been cancelled,
or if by chance he was waiting for the wrong one.
We know, as well, that he would anxiously watch
to see if her luggage would appear on a barrow,
with her following behind, having been delayed.
Those details we know, the ones he wrote down.

2

But what's missing from the picture is the welter
of thoughts in the mind of the man as he stood
alone at the head of a platform curving
into the distance, what he thought as he peered
down the line, hoping she'd swim into view,
one hand on her hat and following her luggage.
What's missing are all those fleeting scenarios
in the mind of a man who kept on strolling
back and forth in the fog while smoking,
flicking at pages but not giving them attention
as he moved around the station and wondered,
Have I met the right train? Will she be on this one?
Some details we know, they were written later.
Everything else going on is as if it never was.

Finding Lines

after CP Cavafy

Ithaca? Well, you know you never actually
get there, never actually arrive?
See, the mere thought of where
you're headed, beyond the horizon,
through dark and light – that's the thing.

Keeping the destination foremost
in mind, and wondering all day
what you might find, will ensure
you don't get lost, won't lose your way,
become distracted or stop and stay.

Diversions are endless, and so you
should be sure to enjoy what you can.
Don't heed the louche gang on Olympus,
a sacrifice or two should sort them out.
And remember, it's you yourself

you most need to be concerned about,
the inner person, the wide-eyed
procrastinator, your ears and nose
inclined to drag you this way and that,
always up and away from the page.

My advice? Well, hope that enough time
goes by to allow a little learning to lodge,
to gain a proper perspective on your purpose.
If you happen to reach your final years
sans the requisite swollen bank balance

or house in some desirable suburb
filled to the brim with accumulated stuff,
don't go getting all bent out of shape.
Such things don't count. Finding lines
is the true concern, day in, day out.

Just *thinking* of Ithaca will be the source
of your wealth. Were it not for the lure
of such a destination, who would set out?
Keep those lines firmly before your eyes
and with them you'll get there, I'm sure.

Ovid in the Cape (a fragment)

He scans the sea, then turns and walks
back into the shuttered room
to gain relief from knives of light.
Dejectedly, he stares at walls,
morosely writes

Three days. Three agonising days
and I am hollowed out.
My breath has slowed to whispering,
my voice become a drawn-out moan.
This body wills – but wills for what, I ask?

A shilling of permission from on high?
I'm stuck; this life, such that it is,
is held within the careless hands
of ever-heartless fate.
How has it come to this?

My story's veered so far from where
I'd thought that I would go,
and now you still see fit
to break all that I am,
to snatch away my very heart...

The sea at night is almost black
and thought torments.
The drill of sleeplessness
keeps him wide awake until
the dawn brings up another day,

far from the smallest shred of home and love.
He drops the pen to cough and wheeze
repeatedly, then slowly walks
from desk to door and out to stand
beside the rail once more.

Three days. Three drawn-out days
of unrelenting heat and wind,
the air an endless rasp
that stings and flays,
chops up the waves and shaves away

the view until it seems the world will end.
Who knows what lies ahead
when thought goes round such fruitless tracks?
That we are authors of our fates
is little more than cruel illusion...

In Which We Examine the Idea of Progress

The old emperor keeps on leaving us,
yet still we long for his easy bonhomie,
for his sonorous and musical words,
his booming voice of unreason.
But now he is no longer with us,
he is gone and the underworld has him,
has his jokes and his firm handshakes,
has his ease with kings and courtesans.

He is gone and the underworld
has him now, has his smile, his manners,
has the long slow look of his eyes
born of years spent in the belly of the law.
We loved him, in a way, as we love
our fathers, believing in their virtues,
caught up in the moment, in the crowds
that fill every square inch of the plaza,

everyone jostling for a view of the man
on the balcony, wanting to be a part
of his smile, his radiance, his eyes,
to be the one acknowledged by his wave.
But the underworld has him now,
and neither memory nor reflection
can return him to us. We loved his ways,
but after one tyrant, comes another.

Now streets are lined and people strew
showers of petals and leaves of silver
picked high on hills and mountain slopes.
Now the streets are sprinkled with drops
from the hands of holy women and men,
now the streets are lined with waiting people.
New emperors, we know, will want
new raiment, will bring with them

their own great family of retainers,
the sycophants and the hangers-on,
experts on canapés and brown envelopes.
And so, the feasting begins, and the dancing,
the swirl of bodies and arms and music,
perfumed oils, the tongues of small birds,
delicate sweetmeats, wines from the south,
the parlaying and the whispered words,

the straying of hands, unbuttoned clothes,
the stroking of breasts and buttocks,
hidden couplings behind long curtains.
The old emperor keeps on leaving us.
How we long for his smile, his bonhomie,
but the underworld has him now
and we must feast and dance and couple
as the new one waves his brave world in.

Paradise

FAURE, *'In paradisum'*

Jan Brueghel's painting, *The Earthly Paradise*,
takes a Hollywood suspension of disbelief:
disinterested lions are lounging around,
rather than leaping with raking claws
onto the back of an antelope standing
alone, unconcerned, staring out of the frame.

It's not what you'd normally expect of a pride
in Africa, say, where teeth and the violent
reduction of others to the status of meat
prevails. Brueghel's suggesting that being
at ease with monkeys and parrots and geese
beneath summer's leaves is all you need.

Perhaps in paradise all creatures are
miraculously maintained in their every
need of sustenance for body and mind.
Perhaps, it implies, unrequitable desire
is the very cause of suffering and misery,
for we, the restless, are barely to be seen.

Such absence suggests we are, *sui generis*,
ourselves the source of all our problems:
the endless discord and discarded bodies,
the non-stop clamour of our disputation.
Despite all the ways in which passing years
have packed in every elaboration,

paradise, it would seem, comes down
to the simple pleasures of uncluttered life
untrammelled by all of our fantasies:
no looking up to beyond the horizon,
or talking oneself into elaborate corners,
no chasing after the latest bright thing

but sitting alone instead in the gloaming
of a summer back garden and listening
to a pipistrelle's soft wings sketching
back and forth across draining light
while knowing in yourself such moments are
about as good as it's ever likely to be.

Strange Daylight

...but the greater part [were] convinced that there were now no gods at all...
PLINY THE YOUNGER

The men in the fields are taking a break,
leaning on hoes while they aimlessly gaze
across late-summer waves of grain towards
the slopes where wisps of cloud keep curling
up the mountain's flanks and around the peak.
This is how it begins, how it always begins.

The ground has shaken twice, before daybreak
and now again, but they pay it no heed.
They have become used to it. One felt a jolt
and woke early, but it left little evidence
except broken tiles and a cracked beam.
The air seems heavy and the light unusual.

One of them lifts a skin to quench his thirst,
wiping his face with a cloth before spitting
and cracking a coarse joke about drink
and gods that sport with the hooved.
They all laugh before returning to hoeing
in silence. The weather has been uncertain

for a week, with none of the full August heat
that's now needed for their crops to ripen.
They sing to the rhythm of their work,
one-two-three-four, *one*-two-three-four...
While they still have air to breathe, they sing,
one-two-three-four, *one*-two-three-four...

This is how it begins, how it always begins.

Poetry as History...

following Geoffrey Hill

Put another way,
you might think of it
as peering at horizons
and wondering what
resurrected fragments
of the past might provide
the right wash of ink

to depict a tongue
that's tied to the faint
flavours of the possible
when looking at what
cannot be spoken of,
cannot but be spoken of.
And yet there is no field

can hold the weight of words,
no ground that's strong enough
to keep the tangled corpse
of what *was* from decomposing
in the very hands of those
whose fate it is to try
and animate the form...

3
SUNDAY

It Takes the Biscuit

The morning's madeleine
has no effect,
not even after
she's carefully dipped
it in a cup.
So, she tries another,
patiently waiting
with a pencil poised
above the sheet.

But nothing happens
throughout the day
except the clicking
arms of clocks
marching steadily,
and quiet breathing
as she listens to
the high, faint drumming
made by molecules

en masse upon
that softest vellum
at the ends of narrowing
trombone-shaped
half-lit passages
tunnelled in-
to the sides of her head
that bring the world
to visit.

Who Now Regards...?

Who now regards the humble buttercup
    glowing at their feet in spring?
Who now will stop and kneel and cherish
    this lovely saffron freely given?

Affairs of state and world bid fair
    to keep us rapt, lost in a maze,
while modest beauty struggles to be
    recognised below our gaze.

Look down, look down, and honour all
    that's small and quiet and ordinary;
let all your substance stop and wonder –
    because they are, you too can be.

Worms

A million hands are waving in the woods nearby.
They flutter in the breeze coming from the east,
growing pale as if they are being starved of light.

Now, it's sad farewell they wave to sunshine as it goes
and heads elsewhere to fall all day on other trees,
on other fields and other plains, on other seas.

Now, the hands fold up and slowly fall to ground.
They gather in half-shaded corners far from wind,
growing fragile, skittish and rustling their complaint.

There's nothing now ahead, they must disintegrate
or be pulled below by worms who've waited in the dark
for beneficent gods to let love rain on them again.

The Tool

It lay undisturbed and out of sight
until rain from a passing summer storm
washed away enough soil to leave
the tool sticking half-in, half-out
where it had long since been abandoned,

having fallen from the grasp of the hand
of the man who was using it when
he heard a faint sound and half-turned,
only to be killed by a blow from behind,
dropping straight down and out of time,

while the killers continued on their way
through the tall grass, leaving the body
to be butchered by the razor-sharp beaks
of winged and ruffed undertakers,
by the heavy and rugged bone-breakers,

by the small and tiny cleaning squads
who left behind an emptied skull
that settled into the mud on the edge
of a lake that was steadily silting up
with the weight of centuries to come.

The Memory of Travel

Later on that morning
he went and sat behind the wheel
and closed his eyes, imagining
that he'd turned the key,
the engine was singing,
and he was busy driving
up and down the Overberg Rûens
on his winding way along
the N2 for PE...

For a while he was happy
each time the horses strained
a little as they climbed a hill
before sweetly angling down
the other side and giving
that slight exhilaration
felt when gravity's hands
are lifted off until
you have to climb again.

And that was it, the thing
he wanted never to end –
the road ahead unfolding
all the way to distant mountains,
to a far-off beating ocean,
to the dry heart in the middle,
to the high, flat plains
and river silted brown
where his life had begun.

Was it the accumulation
of mile after folded mile,
or the filling up of eyes
to the point of saturation,
no intruding thoughts to keep
him out of the present?
The question made him smile,
there never really being any
'because' he knew would fit,

except that in some dim
part of childhood years
an irrepressible delight
in motion was laid down,
the soothing effect of having
scene after scene fly by,
the boundary of images
a fence so wholly able
that it could always keep

his life contained, and calm.

On a Conversation Never Had

i.m. Patricia Gertrude Reid, 1919–84

There was so much more I wished to say
and never did. What was I thinking?
Now, you've gone, and not down the road
for a pint of milk or the daily paper,
for those cigarettes you never could quite
give up despite all best advice
and everything else we knew besides.

There was so much more I wished to know,
and never will. I hadn't the gumption to ask.
What could have been so important to me
to have not been listening for all those years?
Now, all I hear of your voice are echoes
as the memory of you grows steadily fainter
and words keep falling off the page.

There was so much more I wished to hear,
yet never caught when you would explain
why it was throughout your life you'd kept
your hair in tresses, right down to your waist,
or why you'd always made your tea by first
warming the pot and cup with hot water,
carefully measuring spoonfuls from a tin.

There was so much more I wished to grasp
but it didn't stick, and I never quite had
the nous to understand. Now, any chance
has turned to dust, leaving behind
un-had discussions and possibilities,
unspoken words and afternoons unfilled
with clicking needles and gentle chiding.

There was so much more I wished to ask,
and never did; more than I knew to want.
I should have sat quite still through every
available hour until I'd heard it all,
but I never did. Now, there's nothing left
except echoing words, an empty hand,
a departed dream, the draining sand...

Out Shopping

In his bright, neat and new tuxedo,
the smaller bird comically
struts stiff-legged behind his parent,
hoping so to learn exactly
where the choicest morsels lurk.

Each time she takes a turn,
so does he, and when she cocks
an ear to glean if there might be
a busy worm below the green
in easy reach, so does he.

This pattern will be carried on
in time until he's got the hang
of it and knows just how to feed
himself without her presence there.
Day by day, confidence grows.

A magpie's life does not last long.
It's evident where she has worn thin,
is ragged around her neck and head,
lost feathers leaving open patches,
and soon he'll have to shop alone.

His mother will be dead.

Sipping Nectar

The first precision atomic clock
was built in 1955
by Louis Essen and Jack Parry.
It was accurate measuring down
to a millionth of a billionth of a second
and worked by counting the number of times

an atom of caesium-133
flipped from one state to another.
Defined this way, a second is the time it takes
for nine thousand, one hundred and ninety-two million,
six hundred and thirty-one thousand,
seven hundred and seventy spin flips

to have happened in your atom,
which on any one day is much the same time
as an Amethyst Woodstar hummingbird
requires for the eighty wingbeats that keep
it hovering in place and sipping nectar
from a delicate floral trombone.

Thirty-Four South, Eighteen East

"...it feels like standing
on the edge of the world."
JM LEUW

If you pause awhile and stand
in the buffeting wind, all alone
on a hundred million years of stone,
high in the air above the strand,

away from rising-falling waves,
beyond the mouths of carved-out caves,
you get to sense what's going on:
the grinding sand-and-pebble song,

the non-stop lathing by salt wind,
the water wearing rocks away,
the mind's soft cladding slowly thinned
until that point when you might say

that daylight clear is almost showing
through for you to once more see
the insignificance of our being
framed by that deep and musical beat

that keeps on playing: repeat, repeat.

Late Song

Knowing now as you now know
what you'd had no inkling of back then
could always be a reason for regret

were you to think it might have been
much better, say, to have been able
to observe a different self back then

staring back from the room you were in
when looking behind the mirror's sheen –
that it might have been much better, say,

to have lived inside some other being,
to have been a different there and then,
to have been alive elsewhere, else-when,

to have existed in another dream –
knowing now that as a consequence
you'd not be in this when you're in,

you'd not be as you are now being,
you'd not be where you can now see
into the room behind the sheen,

able to look just as you're doing,
and able to say in just this way
that *this* is the sum of everything

recollected and forgotten...
knowing that most of what you've been
has slipped into eternity,

that everything becomes as air,
the fictions and the vagaries
that filled the space you were right there,

that occupied the time of then
when looking at the room behind
the mirror's sheen where everything

– your dreams, desires and memories –
must be relinquished constantly
to get a constant life to sing,

to be the you you've always been.

The Room in the Elephant

It's as if there is a switch, he observed,
pressed down and into the *on* position
keeping in being a world that's filled
with all that's seen when sunlight sings –

a red wing chair and dining table,
the kitchen radio playing the news,
a view of the garden through double doors
and the plum tree's gaudy blossoming,

small birds that mass and seem to fritter
their minutes away inside the hedge,
and the ever-so-distant dome of sky
with its always-changing cloudy scenes.

When pressed up into the *off* position,
not for you do they go on happening.

In the Wide and Dark Landscapes of Time

i.m. Chris Mann, 1948–2021

Once word had come that told of breath
and life stopped in their tracks,
that you had slipped away to join
Douglas, Don, and Guy and Syd,
I felt bereft – not for myself
but rather for our country's song
that now has one less voice to sing
of aloes, stones and prayers and myths,
love's echoing depths, and history;
bereft because in all the wide
landscapes of time you were that most
necessary phenomenon:
the heavenly sound of rain that falls
all day on bare, parched soil.

Sunday

I'd so much planned for Sunday,
having earlier read somewhere
the weather would be great.
My desk was empty, clear,
the shopping had been done.
By car, I'd not be all that late;
I'd been before, I knew the way.

I'd so much planned for Sunday—
food and wine, what clothes I'd wear,
a slow, meandering drive,
enjoying the road before getting there,
stepping out and stretching,
all buoyant and alive.
I'd been before, I knew the way.

Now Sunday's here, I cannot stir
or move my legs and arms, a hand.
I've tried to leave my bed but failed,
as if I am now stuck in sand.
My body seems beyond volition
and though I've strived and railed
against such fate, I cannot spur

my legs to stand so I can go
outside to greet the early sun.
Instead, what binds my soul, I sense,
to body and limbs is now undone,
and I must rise into the air
towards the promised recompense,
the saviour's hands and heaven's glow.

NOTES

p. 12, 'A Short Treatise of Mortality'
Epigraph from *Conversations with Joseph Brodsky: A Poet's Journey Through the Twentieth Century*, SOLOMON VOLKOV

p. 20, 'Bricolages'
Epigraph from 'Sweet Nothing', *Hard Night*, CHRISTIAN WIMAN

p. 40, 'A Bedtime Story'
Epigraph from *Conversations (Vol. 1)*, JORGE LUIS BORGES in conversation with OSVALDO FERRARI

p. 42, 'The Cost of Poetry'
Epigraph from *The Making of Poetry*, ADAM NICHOLSON, on the time that Coleridge and Wordsworth spent living close to one another on the edge of the Quantock Hills in Somerset in 1797–8.

p. 48, 'A Riposte'
"If they give you lined paper, write in the other direction."
– attributed to JUAN RAMÓN JIMINÉZ

p. 54, 'Written'
This poem is based on 'Nel fumo', *Satura*, EUGENIO MONTALE

p. 62, 'Paradise'
Sheet music from the final part of 'Requiem Op.48', GABRIEL FAURÉ

p. 64, 'Strange Daylight'
Epigraph from a letter from PLINY THE YOUNGER's letter to
Cornelius Tacitus on Pompeii's destruction by the eruption of
Vesuvius in 79 CE.

p.78, 'Thirty-Four South, Eighteen East'
The geographical location of Cape Point.

POETRY FOR THE PEOPLE

— RECENT RELEASES IN ENGLISH —

Peach Country by Nondwe Mpuma

Jesus Thesis and Other Critical Fabulations by Kopano Maroga
SHORTLISTED FOR THE 2022 NIHSS AWARD FOR BEST POETRY

An Illuminated Darkness by Jacques Coetzee

Still Further: New Poems, 2000–2020 by C.J. Driver

— RECENT RELEASES IN ISIXHOSA —

Ilifa ngu Athambile Masola
WINNER OF THE 2022 NIHSS AWARD FOR BEST POETRY

Unam Wena ngu Mthunzikazi A. Mbungwana

— RECENTLY-AWARD-WINNING TITLES —

All the Places by Musawenkosi Khanyile
WINNER OF THE 2021 NIHSS AWARD FOR BEST POETRY
WINNER OF THE 2020 SOUTH AFRICAN LITERARY AWARD FOR POETRY

Everything is a Deathly Flower by Maneo Mohale
WINNER OF THE 2020 GLENNA LUSCHEI PRIZE FOR AFRICAN POETRY
FINALIST FOR THE 2020 INGRID JONKER PRIZE

Zikr by Saaleha Idrees Bamjee
WINNER OF THE 2020 INGRID JONKER PRIZE

AVAILABLE FROM GOOD BOOKSTORES IN SOUTH AFRICA *&* NAMIBIA
& FROM THE AFRICAN BOOKS COLLECTIVE ELSEWHERE

UHLANGAPRESS.CO.ZA

Printed in the United States
by Baker & Taylor Publisher Services